MAMA DUCK'S SURPRISE

Mary Alice Umstott Lewis

Archway Publishing books may be ordered through booksellers or by contacting:

Archway Publishing
1663 Liberty Drive
Bloomington, IN 47403
www.archwaypublishing.com
1 (888) 242-5904

Because of the dynamic nature of the Internet, any web addresses or links contained in this book may have changed since publication and may no longer be valid. The views expressed in this work are solely those of the author and do not necessarily reflect the views of the publisher, and the publisher hereby disclaims any responsibility for them.

Any people depicted in stock imagery provided by Getty Images are models, and such images are being used for illustrative purposes only.
Certain stock imagery © Getty Images.

ISBN: 978-1-4808-8364-2 (sc)
ISBN: 978-1-4808-8365-9 (e)

Print information available on the last page.

Archway Publishing rev. date: 10/07/2019

MAMA DUCK'S
SURPRISE

Dedicated to TRAJ

Once there was a little girl, just
about your age. Her name was Majen.
She lived on a farm called
"The Shadows"

There were many animals on the farm,
But Majen's favorite was Mama Duck. Every
Spring, Mama Duck would sit on her eggs,
Which were in a secret nest in the barn.
Mama Duck would have to sit on her eggs
for about five weeks before little ducklings
would hatch. One summer, after Mama Duck had

been on her nest for about three weeks, Majen
found a broken shell beside the nest. Curious
to know why, Majen gently felt and looked
under Mama Duck to see what had happened. A
new baby was under Mama Duck – but it was not
yellow, as a duckling would be. It did say
"Peep peep," but it was black. It was a baby chicken!

A hen had laid her egg in Mama Duck's
Nest and it had hatched. The baby chick
Did not know its warm mother was a duck. It
Was cozy under Mama Duck and the baby chick
Was happy. As it grew, it became bold, and
Ran around the nest and the barn. Often it
Would sit on Mama Duck's back, to keep her
company. Mama Duck was patient with the
chick and they talked to each other. At
night the chick would snuggle under Mama Duck
to keep warm. Of course, Mama Duck was still
very busy with her duck eggs. She talked
to them and carefully turned them every day.

Finally, one day, the chick could hear
"Peep, peep" coming from the eggs. The baby
Ducklings were ready to hatch. It was hard
Work to peck a hole in the shell and break
The shell, but finally Mama Duck had five
Ducklings – and one chick. The ducklings
were very tired and slept while their feathers
dried. They looked like yellow fluff balls
when Majen came to see them that evening.

The next day, Mama Duck decided it was time to
take her babies to the watering pan which Majen
kept nearby. All the ducklings jumped into
the water and floated. They were so happy.
But the chick would not get into the water.
He would only drink of the water. Mama
Duck was puzzled by this strange baby of hers.

Mama Duck took good care of all her Babies.
The chick and the ducklings grew and grew.
They slept in the old nest at night, under Mama
Duck, but soon they were so big she could not cover
them all, even with her wings stretched out.

The babies grew and grew. They began to get white feathers - all except the chick - whose new feathers were black. Finally, the babies were just about fully grown. They still all slept in the barn, on the hay, beside Mama Duck.

Now there was a house for the chickens at the farm, but the new black chicken (who was a hen) did not go into the house. She did not know she was a chicken. She thought she was a duck, even though her voice was now different from the ducks' voices. The hen did know she was not comfortable sleeping on hay at night. Finally, one night, she was not in the barn with the ducks at bedtime. Majen looked and looked for the black hen, and feared a fox might have carried her away. At last Majen found the black hen roosting near the top of pine tree. Now the black hen felt comfortable, roosting with her toes curled around a pine branch. The hen visits the ducks often in the daytime, but at night, Majen can always find her in the pine tree.

Printed in the United States
By Bookmasters